PIANO • VOCAL • GUITAR

T R A I N

MY PRIVATE NATION

ISBN 0-634-06671-4

7777 W. BLUEMOUND RD. P.O. BOX 13819 MILWAUKEE, WI 53213

Visit Hal Leonard Online at
www.halleonard.com

In Australia Contact:
Hal Leonard Australia Pty. Ltd.
22 Taunton Drive P.O. Box 5130
Cheltenham East, 3192 Victoria, Australia
Email: ausadmin@halleonard.com

CONTENTS

CALLING ALL ANGELS

Words and Music by PAT MONAHAN,
SCOTT UNDERWOOD, JAMES STAFFORD
and CHARLIE COLIN

I need a sign ___ to let me know you're here. ___

___ All of these lines ___ are be - ing crossed ___ o - ver the at -

- mos - phere. ___ I need to know ___ that things are gon - na look up ___

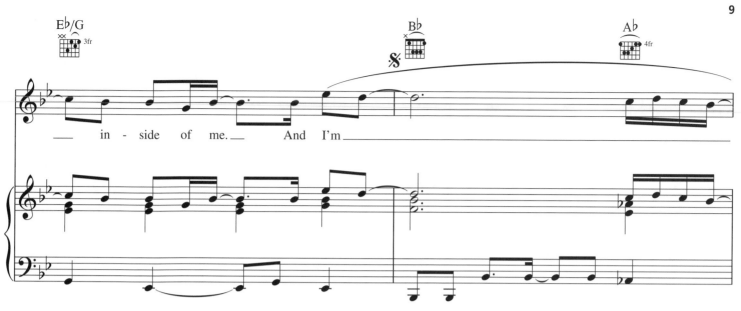

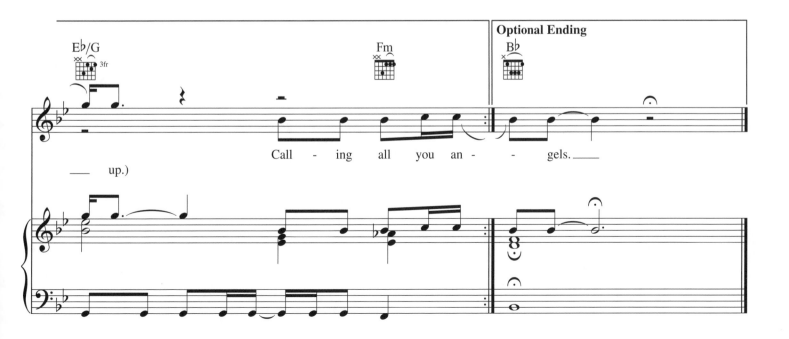

ALL AMERICAN GIRL

Words and Music by PAT MONAHAN
and BRENDAN O'BRIEN

bet you won't say you get cra - zy,   or that you don't shave your legs when you're la - zy,   or that you're

D.S.al Coda

just like ev - 'ry - bod - y else in the world. You just got luck - y, that's____ all.

CODA

The All____ A - mer - i - can Girl.____

The all_____ a -

maz - ing_____ cra - zy girl.____

WHEN I LOOK TO THE SKY

Words and Music by PAT MONAHAN,
SCOTT UNDERWOOD, JAMES STAFFORD
and CHARLIE COLIN

SAVE THE DAY

Words and Music by PAT MONAHAN
and BRENDAN O'BRIEN

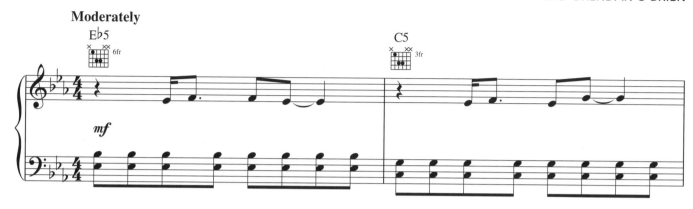

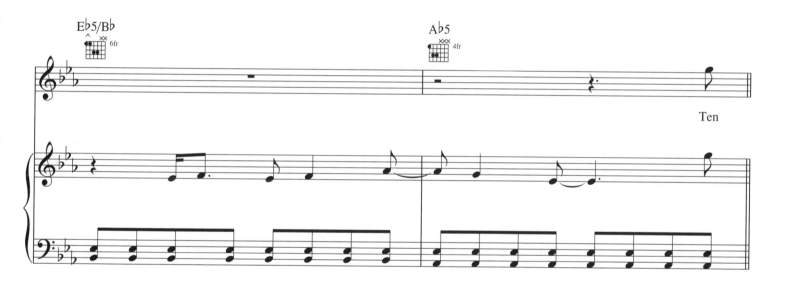

Ten

pounds too much to the na-ked eye.__ I don't take the bus be-cause__ she drives.

I know you don't see me like a mov - ie star.___ And it can't help much that I don't have no car.___ But you're___ my fav - 'rite thing___ by far.___ That's got - ta count for some - thin'. Hey___ ba - by, I___

MY PRIVATE NATION

Words and Music by PAT MONAHAN
and BRENDAN O'BRIEN

GET TO ME

Words and Music by PAT MONAHAN,
SCOTT UNDERWOOD, JAMES STAFFORD,
CHARLIE COLIN and ROBERT HOTCHKISS

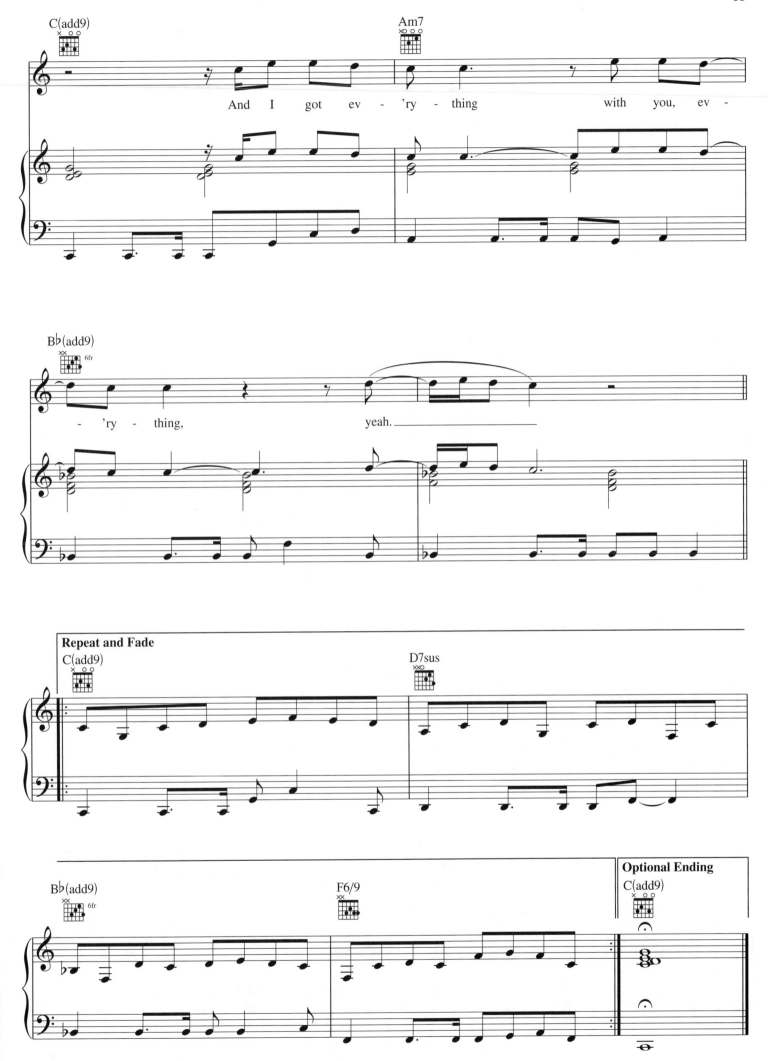

COUNTING AIRPLANES

Words and Music by PAT MONAHAN,
SCOTT UNDERWOOD, JAMES STAFFORD,
CHARLIE COLIN and ROBERT HOTCHKISS

FOLLOWING RITA

Words and Music by PAT MONAHAN,
SCOTT UNDERWOOD, JAMES STAFFORD,
CHARLIE COLIN and ROBERT HOTCHKISS

YOUR EVERY COLOR

Words and Music by PAT MONAHAN,
SCOTT UNDERWOOD, JAMES STAFFORD,
CHARLIE COLIN and ROBERT HOTCHKISS

LINCOLN AVENUE

Words and Music by PAT MONAHAN,
SCOTT UNDERWOOD, JAMES STAFFORD,
CHARLIE COLIN and ROBERT HOTCHKISS

I'M ABOUT TO COME ALIVE

Words and Music by PAT MONAHAN, SCOTT UNDERWOOD,
JAMES STAFFORD, CHARLIE COLIN,
ROBERT HOTCHKISS and CLINT BENNETT

Lyrics:

I can hear ___ you down - stairs ___ cry - ing on ___ the phone ___
tell - ing some - one that I'm here ___ but you still feel all a - lone. ___